The BIG BUCK Adventure

$helley Gill and
Deborah Tobola

Illu$trated by
Grace Lin

Charlesbridge

First paperback edition 2002
Text copyright © 2000 by Shelley Gill and Deborah Tobola
Illustrations copyright © 2000 by Grace Lin

Published by Charlesbridge
85 Main Street, Watertown, MA 02472
(617) 926-0329
www.charlesbridge.com

Library of Congress Cataloging-in-Publication Data
Gill, Shelley.
The big buck adventure/Shelley Gill and Deborah Tobola; illustrated by Grace Lin.
p.   cm.
Summary: Rhyming account of a little girl's quandary as she tries to decide what
she can get with her dollar in a candy shop, toy store, deli, and pet department.
ISBN-13: 978-0-88106-294-6; ISBN-10: 0-88106-294-4 (reinforced for library use)
ISBN-13: 978-0-88106-295-3; ISBN-10: 0-88106-295-2 (softcover)
1. Mathematics Juvenile literature. 2. Money Juvenile literature.
[1. Mathematics. 2. Money.] I. Tobola, Deborah. II. Lin, Grace, ill. III. Title.
QA40.5.G55   2000
513—dc21   99-13393

Printed in Korea
(hc) 10 9 8 7 6 5 4
(sc) 10 9 8 7 6 5 4 3 2

Illustrations done in gouache on Canson watercolor paper
Display type and text type set in Stone Sans and Myriad Tilt
Color separations by Eastern Rainbow, Derry, New Hampshire
Printed and bound by Sung In Printing, South Korea
Production supervision by Brian G. Walker
Designed by Diane M. Earley

To my pop, John Gill, who always knew the value of a buck
—S. G.

To Courtney Heard and her little purple purse
—D. T.

For my dad, who no longer has any big bucks because he spent them all on me
—G. L.

Saturday morning, I sure am in luck!
A raise in allowance—I get a buck!

Dad drops me at the store
with a new green bill.
He says, "I'll be back at a quarter 'til."

I rush to the candy counter,
my head held high.
I flash my moola.
"Please, what can this buy?"

Mr. Cash squints his eyes,
then straightens his collar.

Why, you could buy a hundred jawbreakers for a dollar!

"Tutti-frutti tongue twisters
cost one penny each
in tangerine, lemon-lime,
melon, and peach."

But I see gummy bears
crammed in a jar,
and I ask Mr. Cash
how much those are.

"Three for a quarter, kid,
one for a dime.
You can figure it out.
Just take your time."

Four quarters times three equals
twelve gummy bear treats,
a much better deal
than ten at ten cents each.

Over in toys I spy skates,
trains, and tracks,
rings and stilts and
sets of jacks.

I've got my eye on
a funny stuffed bunny,
but Miss Silver says,

Sorry, not enough money.

$5.

How about a half-dozen creepy night crawlers?
on sale right now—six for a dollar!

I dart into the deli
with a fistful of dough
to see where else
my money can go.

"Howdy, Ms. Penny. What can I buy?"
"Ooh! How 'bout a slice of hot apple pie?

One shiny nickel,
a giant dill pickle!

One quarter, beef jerky.

Three quarters,
leg o' turkey."

In the pet department
there's a plant that eats flies,
and a fuzzy white rat with
black feet and pink eyes.

Mr. Buck has three guppies
for one dollar bill.
He wants eighty-five cents
for ants and a hill.

"Don't want to spend that much?
How about a pet flea
                    or fly
                        or such?

They're three for a penny,
        not a cent more—
            Best doggone deal
                in the whole darn store!"

I figure the math:
thirty-three cents for each fish.
One hundred times three—
more fleas than I wish!

I leave Mr. Buck with
his fleas and his flies
and go stand in housewares
and close my eyes.

Now I wish I didn't have
so much money.
At first this was fun,
now it's not even funny!

What to choose?
One hundred tongue twisters,
tangerine and peach?
Or ten sticky gummy bears
at ten cents each?

Six worms or some jerky?
Three guppies or turkey?

Ants for three quarters
and two nickels?
Or all my cash
for twenty giant pickles?

I've had it.

I can't stand it.

I can't take any more!

I know I'm supposed
to behave in a store,

But I stride to the middle
of the place, and I holler,
"What in the world should
I buy with my dollar?"

They come running:
Cash, Silver, Buck, and Penny.
Clutching my bill I yell,

I don't want

My head is spinning with what
I could have bought

When Miss Silver asks,

Penny for your thoughts?

Slowly I turn and say like a scholar,
"Why you can have one hundred
of my thoughts for a dollar!

Ten thoughts for a dime,
five for a nickel,
twenty-five thoughts
for five sour dill pickles.

Three for a quarter
is not the best deal,

but flea-thoughts
and fly-thoughts   are really a steal!"

My father walks in.

Hi, honey! Any luck?

I just have to laugh
as I pocket my buck.

LITERACY PLACE®

HYMAN FINE SCHOOL

Hello!

Copyright acknowledgments and credits appear on page 104, which constitutes an extension of this copyright page.

Copyright © 2000 by Scholastic Inc.   All rights reserved   Printed in the U.S.A.

ISBN 0-439-06138-5

4 5 6 7 8 9 10   09   05 04 03 02 01 00

TABLE OF CONTENTS

THEME
We share what we like.

UNIT 1

Author/Illustrator
Brian Wildsmith

Brian Wildsmith loves to paint bright, bold animals like the ones in the <u>Cat on the Mat</u>. He says that animals can teach us many things. He also says that we should try to do what we love to do best. If we love to do something, we will do it well.

Cat

on the Mat

Written and Illustrated by Brian Wildsmith

The cat sat on the mat.

The dog sat on the mat.

The goat sat on the mat.

The cow sat on the mat.

The elephant

14

sat on the mat.

Ssspppstt!

The cat sat on the mat.

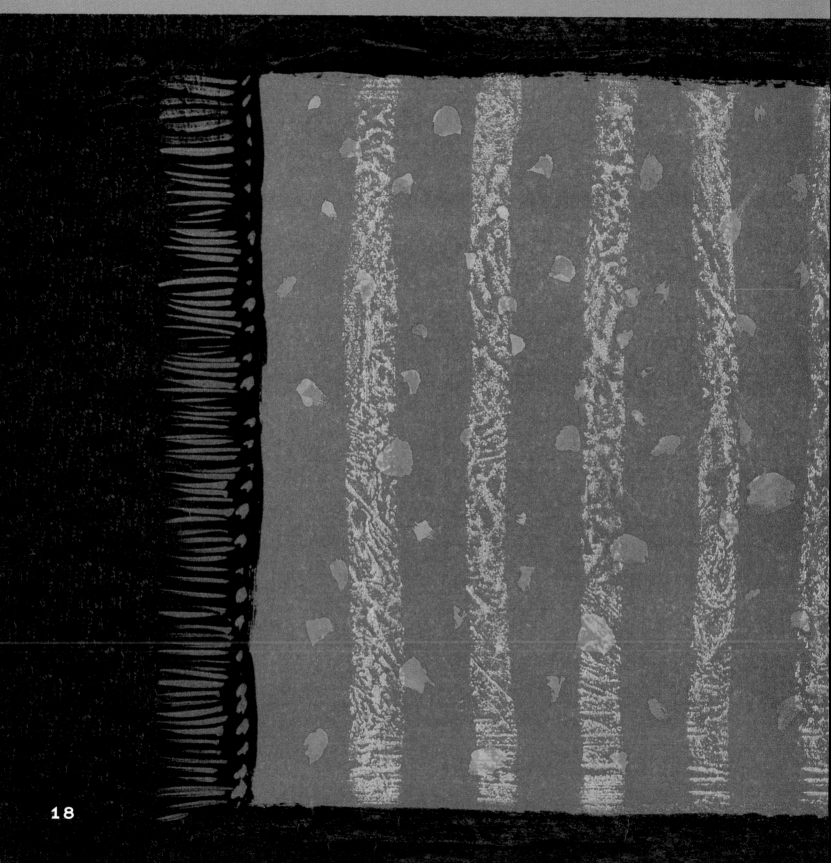

PRE-DECODABLE:
KINDERGARTEN
TRANSITION

ABC, What Can

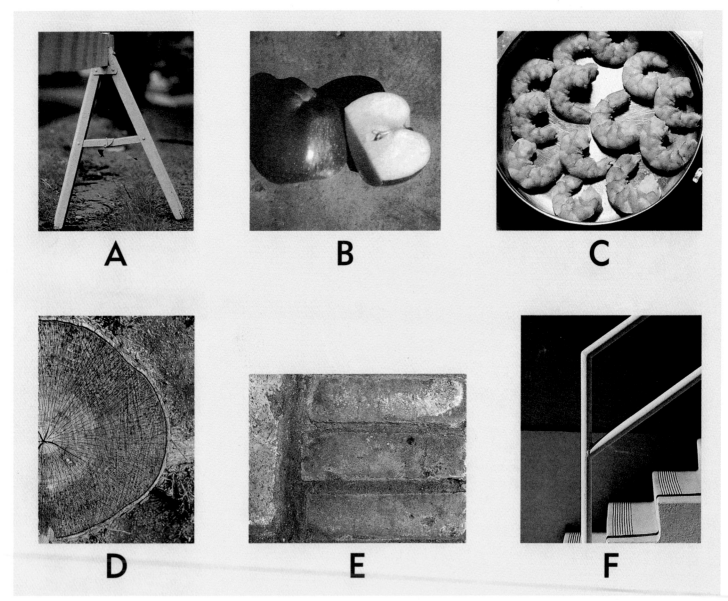

A

B

C

D

E

F

I see an A.
What can you see?

You See? photos by Arlene Alda

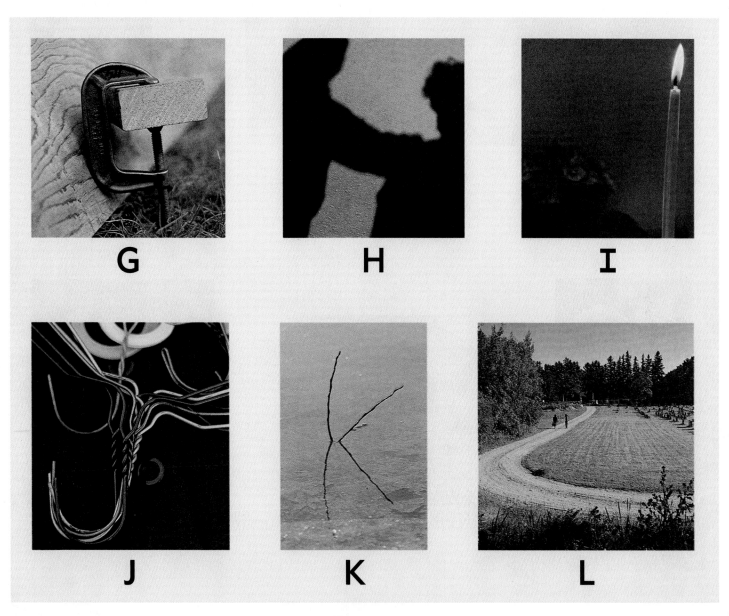

G

H

I

J

K

L

I see an I.
What can it be?

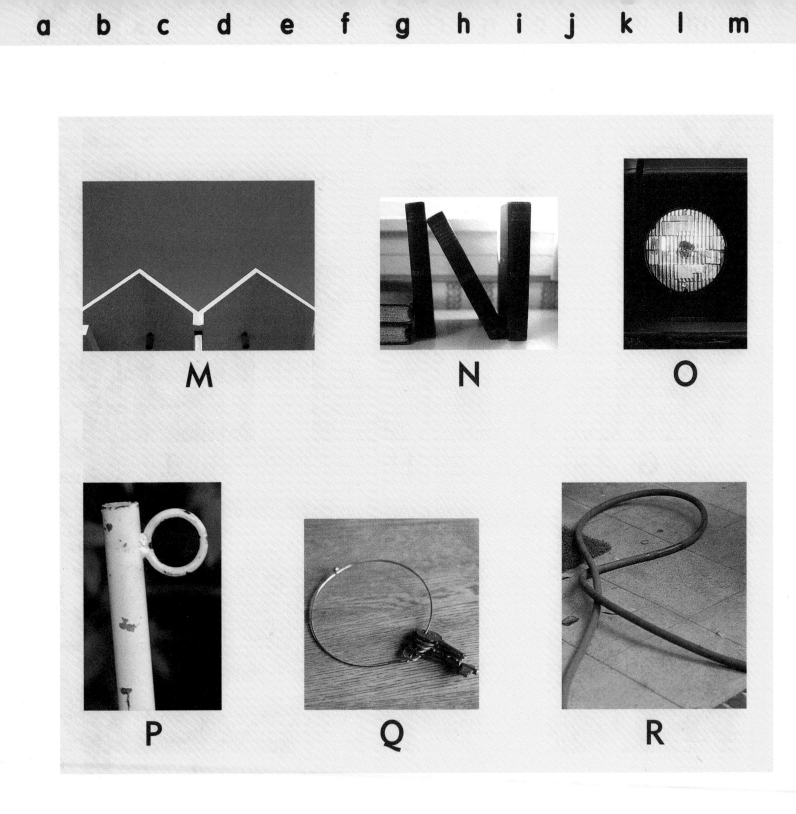

M

N

O

P

Q

R

I see an O.
I see a P.

S

T

U

V

W

X

Y

Z

I see an S.
Can you see the Z?

Author
Jesús Cervantes

Jesús Cervantes grew up on a ranch. His love of books came from stories his mother would tell him from her childhood in Mexico. Now he is a teacher, a writer, and a storyteller, too.

Let's Go!

written by
Jesús Cervantes

photographs by
Richard Hutchings

I go on a big bike.
Where will I go?

I go with my mom.

Where will I go?

I go in a car.

Where will I go?

I go in a cab.

Where will I go?

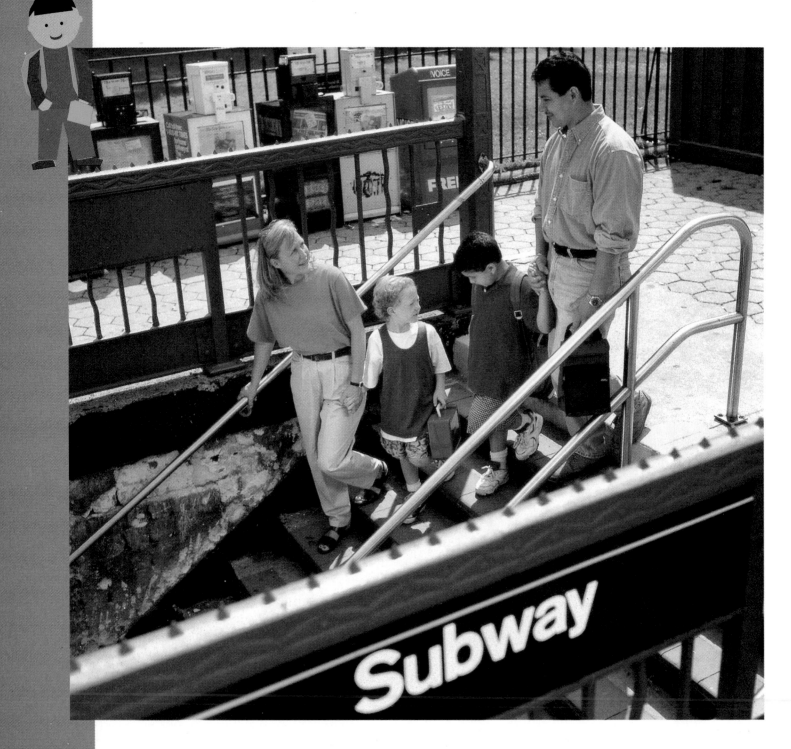

I go on the subway.

Where will I go?

I go on a van.

Where will I go?

I go on a bus.

Where will I go?

To school!
We all go to school.

Chapter 2

We see our teacher at school.

Hello!

We sit on the mat and read.

We sit and write.

We play a lot.
We go up and down.

We sing.

We hop.

We paint.
We mop.

We read a lot.

Time to go.
Goodbye!

📖 Read Together!

Donald Crews

Author/Illustrator

Donald Crews writes books for children. He writes about things he sees and likes. Donald Crews also draws the pictures to go with his stories.

SCHOOL

One of his most popular books is <u>School Bus</u>. This book tells the story of how many children go to school.

Donald Crews likes to draw himself in his books. Can you find him in this picture from <u>School Bus</u>?

Author/Illustrator
Monica Wellington

As a child, Monica Wellington lived near mountains, lakes, fields, and farms, and drew pictures of what she saw. She still likes to draw different kinds of places filled with colorful details. They remind her of her happy childhood.

What

Music
Shop

MAIL

by
Monica Wellington

I am Jan.

I like many things.

I like my cat.

I like mice, too.

We like to play on the mat.

I like the drums.

Rat-a-tat-tat. Rat-a-tat-tat.

The man plays a drum.

48 I like to play, too.

I like hats.

Big hats. Little hats.

I like lots of hats.

I like cakes.

Pat-a-cake. Pat-a-cake.

I like to make cakes.

I like to read.

I like to write.

I like lots and lots of books.

I like to see the moon.
I like the stars, too.
I like the sky at night.

I like many things.
What do you like?

We Like

by Children of the U.S.A.

I like my cat.

It is fat.

by Arin Higginbotham

I like my ant.

It is little and red.

by Marissa Miller

I like my fish.
It is big.
It can swim.

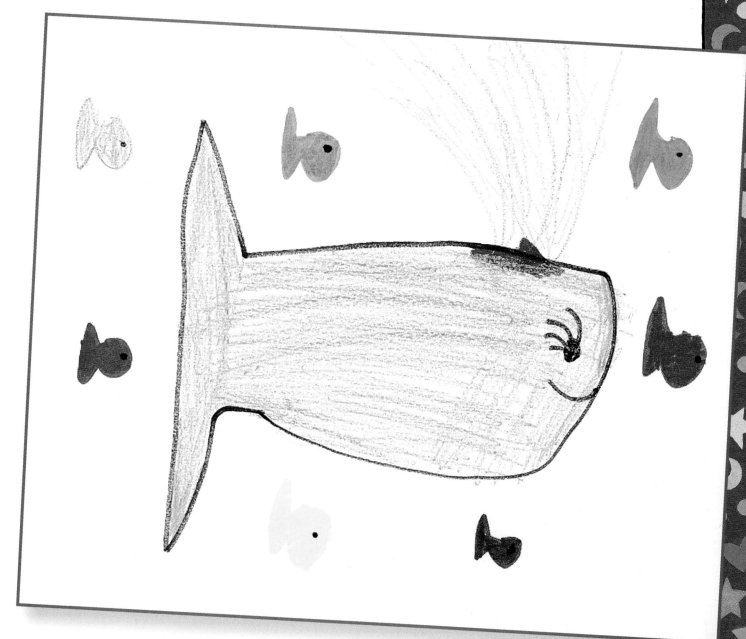

by Adina Dupré

I like to dance.

Do you?

by Vesenia Rivera

I like to hop.

I can jump, too.

by Jessica Gallegos

I like my school a lot.

I like to read and play at school.

by Jolene Ramos

I like to sit on my mom's lap.

Here I am.

I love my mom!

by Kristen Sanchez

HOP ON POP

By Dr. Seuss

HOP
POP

We like to hop.
We like to hop
on top of Pop.

STOP

You must not
hop on Pop.

Author
Angela Shelf Medearis

Angela Shelf Medearis
moved often while growing
up. She soon discovered
that favorite books were
like good friends who would
be waiting for her at the
library of every new town.
Even now, her favorite
books are children's books.

Peanut

Butter and Jam

written by Angela Shelf Medearis

illustrated by Barry Rockwell

JAM

Peanut Butter

**Chapter 1
JAM**

"Do you want some toast?" said Pam.

"Yes, I do," said Dan.
"I like toast with peanut butter."

"I like jam on toast," said Pam.

"We do not have jam," said Dan.
"I'll have to go to the store in my van."

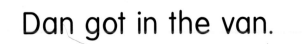

Dan got in the van.

Dan got to the store.
But Dan forgot what Pam said.

"What do you want?" said Sam.

"Pam likes . . ." said Dan.

"What is it?" said Sam.
"A hat? A cat? A pan? A fan?
A ham? Or a ram?"

"That is it!" said Dan.
"Pam wants a ram."

Dan got in the van.

The ram sat in the van with Dan.

"I got the ram," said Dan.

"Not ram, silly!" said Pam.

"I said JAM."

"I want jam on my toast."

"I forgot," said Dan.

"I'll go back to the store in my van."

Chapter 2
PEANUT BUTTER

Dan went back to the store.
But Dan forgot what Pam said.

"Pam likes . . ." said Dan.

"What do you want?" said Sam.
"A mop? A top? A mat? A hat?"
"A ham? Or a pot of jam?"

"Jam! That is it!" said Dan.
"I want a pot of jam."

75

"That is a BIG pot of jam," said Dan.

"Yes, it is a lot," said Sam.

"The jam will not go in my van," said Dan.

"We can put the jam on top," said Sam.

"What is that?" said Pam.

"A pot of jam," said Dan.

"Good!" said Pam.

"I like a lot of jam," said Pam.

"And I like peanut butter," said Dan.

"We do not have peanut butter," said Pam.

JAM

78

"You are silly!" said Dan.

"We like to be silly," said Pam.

"Yes, we do!" said Dan.

from

Read Together!

Now We Are Six

by A. A. Milne
illustrated by
Ernest H. Shepard

The End

When I was One,
I had just begun.

When I was Two,
I was nearly new.

When I was Three,
I was hardly Me.

When I was Four,
I was not much more.

When I was Five,
I was just alive.

But now I am Six, I'm as clever as clever.
So I think I'll be six now for ever and ever.

Dots!

Author
Francie Alexander

Francie Alexander says Dots! Dots! Dots! was fun to write because looking at art is fun to do. Writing this book gave her the chance to tell about some of her favorite paintings. The painting called "Little Red House" hangs in her own home and inspired her to write this story.

Dots! Dots!
At the Museum

by
Francie Alexander

The Postman Roulin, Vincent Van Gogh

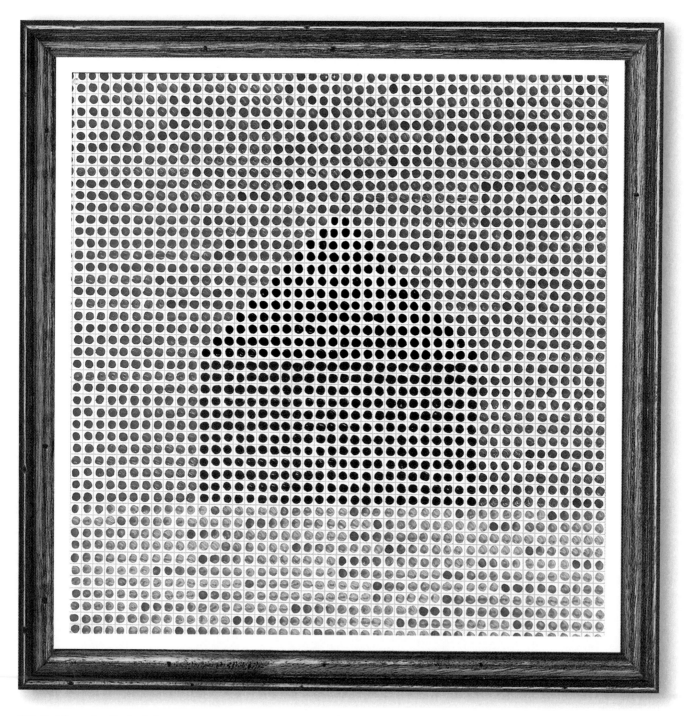

Little Red House, Jennifer Bartlett

Dots! Dots! Dots!

I see lots of dots.

What do you see?

A House

Jumping Rope, Arinthia L. Jones

I see girls hop, hop, hop.

I see dots on the girls.

What do you see?

Buttons

Impression: Sunrise, Claude Monet

I see a dot.

It is up in the sky.

It looks hot.

What is it?

The Sun

Bottlecap Giraffe, Anonymous

I see something big with dots.

It can run.

What can it be?

A
Giraffe

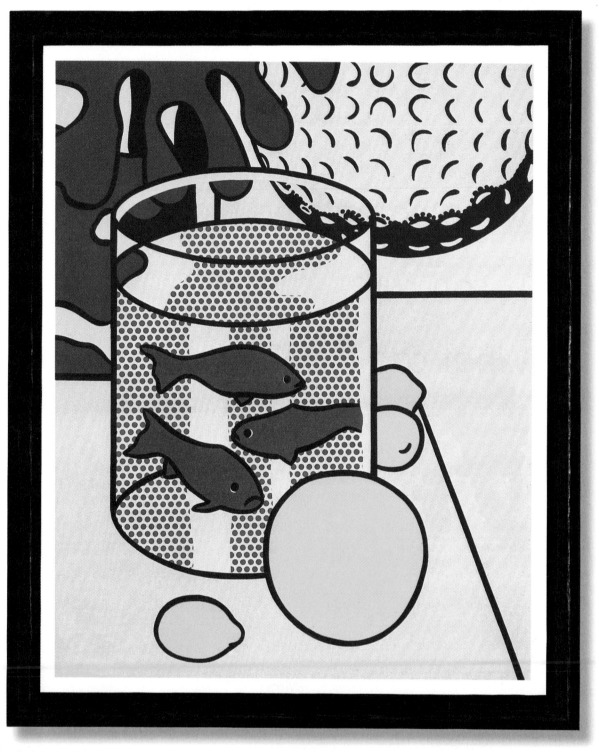

Still Life with Goldfish Bowl, Roy Lichtenstein

Dots! Dots! Dots!

I see a lot of blue dots.

What do you see?

Water

Piñata, Diego Rivera

I see something pop.

Pop, pop, pop!

It has lots of dots.

What do you see?

A Piñata

The Girls, Christian Pierre

98

I see lots of black dots.

I do not see a cat.

What do I see?

Dogs

Senecio, Paul Klee

Dots! Dots! Dots!

I see two red dots.

Can the dots see me?

What can you see?

A Man

Reflections

by Myra Cohn Livingston
illustrated by Melissa Sweet

In the mirror
I can see
Lots of things
But mostly—me.

WORD LIST

m

ham	mom
jam	mop
man	Pam
mat	ram

l

lap	lot

s

cats	hats
dots	sat

a

am	Jan
an	lap
ants	man
at	mat
can	Pam
cat	pan
Dan	pat
fan	ram
hat	rat
ham	sat
jam	van

t

at	mat
cat	not
dot	pat
got	pot
hat	rat
hot	sat
lot	top

o

dot	mop
got	not
hop	pop
hot	pot
lot	top
mom	

········· High-Frequency Words ·········

a	I	my	the
and	in	of	to
be	is	on	we
do	it	said	what
go	like	see	you

Acknowledgments

Grateful acknowledgment is made to the following sources for permission to reprint from previously published material. The publisher has made diligent efforts to trace the ownership of all copyrighted material in this volume and believes that all necessary permissions have been secured. If any errors or omissions have inadvertently been made, proper corrections will gladly be made in future editions.

"Cat on the Mat" from CAT ON THE MAT by Brian Wildsmith. Copyright © 1982 by Brian Wildsmith. Reprinted by permission of Oxford University Press.

SCHOOL BUS by Donald Crews. Copyright © 1984 by Donald Crews. By permission of Greenwillow Books, a division of William Morrow & Co., Inc.

"Hop on Pop" from HOP ON POP by Dr. Seuss. TM and copyright © 1963 by Dr. Seuss Enterprises, L.P. Reprinted by permission of Random House, Inc.

"The End" from NOW WE ARE SIX by A. A. Milne, illustrations by E. H. Shepard. Copyright © 1927 by E. P. Dutton, renewed © 1955 by A. A. Milne. Reprinted by permission of Dutton Children's Books, a division of Penguin Putnam Inc.

"Reflections" from A SONG I SANG TO YOU by Myra Cohn Livingston. Copyright © 1984, 1969, 1967, 1965, 1958, 1959 by Myra Cohn Livingston. All copyrights renewed. Reprinted by permission of Marian Reiner.

Photography and Illustration Credits

Photos: p. 4, Courtesy Oxford University Press; pp. 20–23: Arlene Alda; p. 24, Courtesy Jesús Cervantes; pp. 25–41, Richard Hutchings for Scholastic Inc.; p. 42, Halley Ganges for Scholastic Inc.; p. 44, Courtesy Monica Wellington; p.54, Peter Correz for Tony Stone Images; p. 64, Bob Daemmerich for Scholastic Inc.; p. 84, David Blasband; p. 85, Künsthaus, Zurich, Switzerland/ Giraudon, Paris/ SuperStock; p. 86, Joseph Sinnott / by Permission Jennifer Bartlett; p. 88, Arinthia L. Jones / Ethnographics; p. 90, Musee Marmottan, Paris/ Bridgeman Art Library/ Christie's Images; p. 92, National Museum of American Art / Art Resource, NY.; p. 94, Estate of Roy Lichtenstein; p. 96, Hospital Infantil de Mexico; p. 98, Private Collection/ Christian Pierre/ SuperStock; p. 100, Künstmuseum, Basel, Switzerland. Giraudon/ Art Resource. NY.

Cover: Barry Rockwell for Scholastic Inc.

Illustrations: pp. 44–53: Monica Wellington for Scholastic Inc. pp. 64–81: Barry Rockwell for Scholastic Inc. pp. 84–101: Nancy Davis for Scholastic Inc. p. 102: Melissa Sweet for Scholastic Inc.

Illustrated Author Photos: pp. 4, 24, 44, 64, 84: David Franck for Scholastic Inc.